Endorsements

"Enjoying Agile and My Job is a great book and has helped reignite and recenter myself around the things that truly matter in my work and business operations. In his book, Akeloe does an excellent job in asking powerful questions around the core things that matter, causing the reader to pause and think introspectively about how they are approaching challenges, and how they might improve their approach...This book helped me see how I can improve and provide folks with the best and most loving work environment possible."

— **Skipper Davies,** Principal Consultant and Owner, Agile Consulting Advisers LLC

"Enjoying Agile and My Job is a labor of love by someone who has lived it for over a decade. Akeloe Facey delivers this resource with people in mind, not simply the end user or customer, but the leader, professional, and Agilist. As the goal of this guide is to inform, inspire, and motivate people, it is deliberately not written in the lofty pedagogy of academia. Instead, it is delivered in simple, practical, and easy to digest nuggets of information, woven together by both generally accepted practices and faith-based resources, to provide a holistic perspective on the value of Agile principles. Allow this book to be your companion as you grow to work smarter, faster, and more efficiently, never forsaking the most important part of the equation: the people."

—**Christian Hicks MBA,** Recruiter, Penn State

"Enjoying Agile and My Job is a book I wish I could have referenced in my earlier career when I was introduced to Agile. This book is a must read for the old and new Agilist. The book focuses on the 12 principles of Agile with a mindset of purpose, conviction, vision and passion."

—**Davon Nasir,** Program Director, Universal
Service Administrative Company

"This is an impassioned book written by an Agilist directed at any experience level of Agile contributor. With many professional development books filled with only high-level theoretical approaches it was refreshing to have a philosophical approach to driving organizational success that was supported by a flexible blueprint to model after. "From Purpose to Inspiration", Mr. Facey shares the knowledge to bring excitement and fulfillment to your job and equips you with the tools to get the most out of you and your professional relationships."

—**Jamie Clayton,** Senior Software Engineer, Hillrom

"After reading the book I was able to connect how the Agile Principles can help with my organization to reach its unique goals and to create a vision and a road-map for achieving them. I'm able to better understand the source of people's resistance and build a strategy to help bring them along on the journey to realizing the true benefits of Agile."

—**Floris Dafel,** Scrum Master, NTT

"This book should be read by every person tasked with ensuring teams are in alignment with the Agile principles. I particularly like the 17 qualities and practices for a Scrum Master. It provides a roadmap to excellence in the discipline."

—**Cherrie Reid, PMP PMI-ACP, SAFe,** Project Manager

"This is a great read about someone who knows Agile in and out. The study questions will prompt the Agilist to think about their own journey. It's really engaging and motivating."

—**Jaron Cunningham,** President, The Jacy Method

"I love how interactive the book is, it opens the reader's mind to think a little bit deeper than just "This is my job, and I need to tick the boxes.""

—**Teri Pieterson,** Scrum Master, Wonga

Enjoying Agile and My Job

Cultivating an Attitude that Enjoys, Promotes and Sustains the Agile Principles

AKELOE FACEY PMP, PMI-ACP, CSP

WESTBOW
PRESS®
A DIVISION OF THOMAS NELSON
& ZONDERVAN

WestBow Press books may be ordered through booksellers or by contacting:

WestBow Press
A Division of Thomas Nelson & Zondervan
1663 Liberty Drive
Bloomington, IN 47403
www.westbowpress.com
1 (866) 928-1240

Scriptures taken from the Holy Bible, New International Version®, NIV®. Copyright © 1973, 1978, 1984, 2011 by Biblica, Inc.™ Used by permission of Zondervan. All rights reserved worldwide. www.zondervan.com The "NIV" and "New International Version" are trademarks registered in the United States Patent and Trademark Office by Biblica, Inc.™

ISBN: 978-1-9736-7434-4 (sc)
ISBN: 978-1-9736-7433-7 (e)

Print information available on the last page.

WestBow Press rev. date: 11/11/2019

Contents

Contents

List of Figures

Foreword

Let's be honest. Being the "Agile Advocate" can be exhausting. How can you motivate, inspire and influence when encountering resistance, skepticism and sometimes outright, tyranny?

As an Agilist myself, it is easy to forget "that circumstances do not have to remain as is." Lucky for us, *"Enjoying Agile and My Job: Cultivating An Attitude that Enjoys, Promotes, and Sustains the Agile Principles"* refocuses and reconnects us to what originally sparked our Agile mindset — purpose, conviction, vision, and passion.

I've had the pleasure of working with and witnessing Akeloe's tireless devotion to teaching Agile, coaching towards excellence and influencing organizational culture. Akeloe's positive energy, continual curiosity, and optimism is infectious, both in person and now, through the words on these pages.

This book is an encouraging and motivational read for all struggling Agilists, regardless of experience, role or level. Akeloe is your friend, a gentle guide and guardian who helps you navigate the complex world of Agility. He provides you with real-world experiences, based on his own personal and professional challenges and breakthroughs.

His commitment, authenticity, and passion are unwavering as he challenges the status quo, exploring the subtleties, benefits, and driving influences behind each of the 12 Agile Principles. In this book, Akeloe provides tactical advice that you can use immediately.

Akeloe offers real-world solutions on how to:

- Revive your own commitment and passion for Agile
- Lead from your heart
- Stay true to yourself and your own convictions
- Transition to a more purpose-driven mindset
- Become proficient in your understanding of the 12 Agile Principles
- Identify your team's anti-patterns
- Anticipate situational problems as opportunities for improvement
- Encourage your team members to be more self-organizing and cross-functional

In addition, each chapter includes a list of powerful questions designed to challenge your perceptions and ideas, and allowing you to absorb and contemplate what you just read. This is where I personally gained the most value from the content.

"Enjoying Agile and My Job: Cultivating An Attitude that Enjoys, Promotes, and Sustains the Agile Principles" has inspired me to dive deeper into my craft, so that I can truly connect to my own purpose and passion.

As Akeloe has stated: "Agilists of the world have a purpose of thoroughly understanding, appreciating and embracing the principles of Agile." This book was a fantastic reminder of that and I can honestly say I feel a renewed sense of vigor and excitement.

This Agilist is ready to motivate, inspire and influence. I believe you will be too.

Kimberly Andrikaitis, Agile Coach
www.agile-dork.com

Introduction

"That's not Agile", "What you're doing is anti-Agile," "Hey, stop telling me what to do...that's not Agile, you're doing that command and control thing." As an Agilist, you may hear these statements from time to time. In one planning session, a team wanted to experiment and try something new with how work was assigned to each developer and quality assurance personnel. Someone on the team expressed that this approach the team is taking is anti-Agile. His statement caught me off guard and I had a sneaky suspicion that he didn't know what Agile was. My suspicion was confirmed a few hours later. We had a candid conversation where I explained to him that his rationale for saying that the team's practice was anti-Agile was unfounded. He also acknowledged that he didn't have a strong understanding of Agile. Wow! I immediately thought to myself, "How can you call a line crooked if you don't know what a straight line looks like?" In other words, how can you say something is anti-Agile if you don't know what Agile is? I suspect that these types of episodes probably happen a lot in many organizations.

The Agile Principles, I believe, are not always fully understood in organizations, and because of this misunderstanding many believe that its value is overestimated. So often I hear individuals who are not familiar with Agile make statements such as "they're making us do this Agile stuff; it just doesn't work." Consequently, the potential benefits of embracing and executing these principles are sometimes never realized in the organization. An additional byproduct of this attitude is that the Agilist in the organization may begin to lose his commitment and passion for these principles.

1

Unfortunately, I've witnessed this happen. Such pessimism can potentially cause the Agilist to stop enjoying, promoting and sustaining the Agile Principles. When it gets to this point, the Agilist is doing a disservice to himself and to his organization. I use the term "Agilist" in the same way as Dr. Gaiyasudeen Syed. He defines it as "one who in their business practice acts in a way that reflects the Agile Principles."[1]

The challenges I've described motivated me to write this book. I work in organizations that have made commitments to adopt these principles. Therefore, I want to remind myself and encourage other Agilists to go to work each day to be passionate and consistent in effectively carrying out these principles. See the principles below:

No.	Agile Principles (as defined in the Manifesto)	Agile Principles (in my own words)	Benefits of the Principles (in my own words)
1	Our highest priority is to satisfy the customer through early and continuous delivery of valuable software.	Satisfy customer with valuable software.	To ensure customer retention and continuous business growth.
2	Welcome changing requirements, even late in the development, Agile processes harness change for the customer's competitive advantage.	Welcome change to requirements.	As changes can sometimes lead to a customer's competitive advantage.
3	Deliver working software frequently, from a couple of weeks to a couple of months, with a preference to the shorter timescale.	Deliver working software frequently.	To get feedback early and often to ensure we're building in accordance with the expectations, wants and needs of the customer.
4	Business people and developers must work together daily throughout the project.	Business people and development team should work together.	So that business understands the technical implications of their decisions and the development team understands the business impact of their decisions.
5	Build projects around motivated individuals. Give them the environment and support they need and trust them to get the job done.	Build projects around motivated people.	Building work around motivated people and providing them with autonomy increases the likelihood for success in your projects.
6	The most efficient and effective method of conveying information to and within a development team is face to face conversation.	Promote F2F conversation.	As this allows for the quickest transfer of information between parties.
7	Working software is the primary measure of progress.	Ensure working software is the primary measure of progress.	As this helps to create a results-oriented view of the project.
8	Agile processes promote sustainable development. The sponsors, developers, and users should be able to maintain a constant pace indefinitely.	Promote a sustainable and constant pace.	Helps to give workers a good work/life balance so they don't get burned out.
9	Continuous attention to technical excellence and good design enhances agility.	Ensure continuous attention on technical excellence.	To help keep the design and code clean, efficient and open to change.
10	Simplicity - the art of maximizing the amount of work not done - is essential.	Focus on simplicity.	To ensure we boil requirements down to the essential elements only.
11	The best architectures, requirements and design emerge from self-organizing teams.	Self-organizing teams build the best requirements, design and architecture.	Since they thoroughly understand and support the approach, this increases the likelihood for high quality work due to higher ownership and pride of the work.
12	At regular intervals, the team reflects on how to become more effective, then tunes and adjusts its behavior accordingly.	At regular intervals, fine tune and adjust.	So that we can reflect on how we're doing; and identify opportunities for improvement.

Figure 1: Agile Principles

I know that these principles work; I know that these principles are benefiting my company; I know that there's some correlation with business growth and the application of the Agile Principles. One experience that comes to mind that further validates the effectiveness of these principles occurred when I was working as a Scrum Master for a team that had the responsibility of delivering functionality critical to the organization's mission. It was during that time that I noticed that one of the developers lacked motivation and was undependable. This negatively impacted the team from functioning in accordance with the fifth and eleventh principles of Agile. The lack of motivation from this developer would eventually reduce the likelihood for the team to operate in a self-organizing and self-directing manner. Seeing this anti-Agile behavior prompted me to have a conversation with this developer. I knew that this was a coaching opportunity. I truly value these moments with team members because I have a unique forum and privilege to give them constructive feedback that can help them to thrive as an employee. In my conversation with this developer, I asked her a series of questions regarding competence, commitment and consistency. In our one on one conversation, I asked the following questions:

- Do you perform your work with excellence? How can your team tell? (competence)
- Are you dedicated to the team's success? How can your team tell? (commitment)
- Can you be depended on every time? Are there areas where you're not consistent? (consistency)

Asking these questions allowed me to drive the conversation in a way that would minimize defensiveness and allow her to see the truth about her behavior on her own (people tend to be more receptive to truth when they discover it on their own). It was a very productive conversation as she was both receptive and thankful for the feedback. A few weeks after this conversation, I noticed a positive change in this developer. She went from being one of the most unmotivated people on the team to becoming one of the most dependable and committed individuals on the team. The prompting to discuss and address this concern with the developer occurred primarily because of the recognition that this behavior deviated from the principles. I'm passionate about these principles because they represent a guard rail to help ensure teams are moving towards an Agile mindset, thereby functioning more efficiently. *See Appendix A for helpful tips for coaching teams to become more self-organized.*

Better understanding the work that I do as an Agilist and the positive impact it has on the company's growth has helped me to have a renewed passion for my job. I'm not only saying "Happy Friday", but also "Happy Monday, Tuesday, Wednesday, and Thursday"! In the past, there were times that I asked myself if my role as an Agilist (i.e. Scrum Master, Agile Project Manager) was making much of a difference. I didn't feel as though I was providing much value or significance to the teams I was on. I unfortunately allowed people's low perception of the principles to influence how I viewed the principles and my role. It wasn't until I reminded myself to go back and better understand the fundamentals of why I even promote the Agile Principles that a new excitement and joy for my role started brewing. And it's still brewing. To help with understanding the fundamentals, I placed stickies on the walls of my home office to keep them as a constant refresher and reminder (see Figure 2 below). Additionally, I made a voice recording of the principles on my cell phone and listened to it at least twice a week on my way to work so that I was constantly reminded of the benefits.

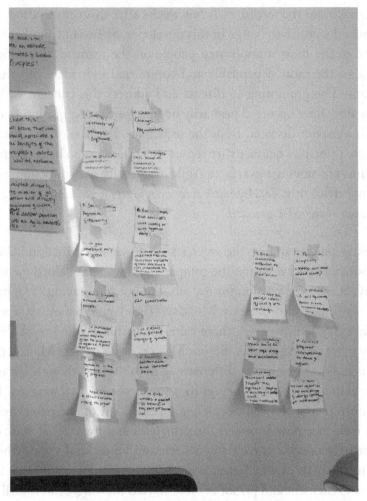

Figure 2: Agile Principles - Home Office

In the past few years, I've seen others go through similar moments. I've noticed that many in this field have lost the passion for or have been discouraged in continuing to promote the Agile Principles. I'm sure there are several reasons for this, but I suspect the primary reasons to be the professed Agilist either (1) lacks strong conviction in promoting these principles, (2) has experienced strong vocal opposition from team members that do not recognize or care about the benefits of Agile, consequently allowing those opinions to discourage them or (3) has an insufficient understanding of the core benefits of each of the Agile Principles. These factors and many others can discourage the best of us. Given this, the aim of this book is to demonstrate that when we embrace the benefits of the Agile Principles and see how the application of these principles support the mission of the organization and directly drives business growth, this will help Agilists cultivate and maintain a deeper and unwavering enthusiasm for their role in the organization.

Lack of passion in the workforce is not limited to the Agilist. Lack of zeal and engagement in one's job has unfortunately become a common thing. Studies are showing that the majority of the modern workforce are not engaged or excited about their jobs. Gallup, an organization that delivers analytics and advice to help leaders and organizations solve their most pressing problems, helped to provide some insight on this issue. Gallup recently completed a study titled 'State of the American Workplace' that was aimed at understanding employees' engagement in the modern workforce. This report was based on extensive work in a variety of industries of over 195,000 employees. The study showed that only 33% of employees are *engaged* at their jobs.[2] That means 67% are either *not engaged* or *actively disengaged.* Let's establish some definitions around these terms:

- Engaged: Employees are highly involved in and enthusiastic about their work and workplace. They are psychological "owners," drive performance and innovation, and move the organization forward.
- Not Engaged: Employees are psychologically unattached to their work and company. Because their engagement

needs are not being fully met, they're putting time - but not energy or passion - into their work.

- Actively Disengaged: Employees aren't just unhappy at work - they are resentful that their needs aren't being met and are acting out their unhappiness. Every day, these workers potentially undermine what their engaged coworkers accomplish.

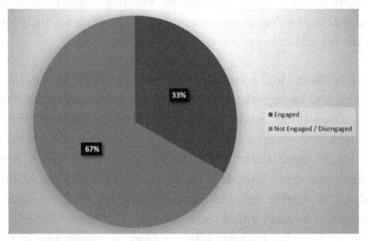

Figure 3: Gallup Study on American Workplace

While the results of the study were not very surprising, they were very disheartening considering that we spend so much time at work. I think about my household for example. We're awake for about 16 hours of the day; and out of those 16 hours, 10 hours are devoted to work (i.e. getting dressed for work, driving to work, functioning at work). So, 63% of my waking hours are devoted to a job (see Figure 3 below). That's a large number, but I'm sure this fails in comparison to others. If I was a part of the 67% of Not Engaged or Actively Disengaged, that means each day I'm consistently devoting most of my waking hours to an organization or role that provides no degree of significance, satisfaction or value. The encouraging thing is that the report doesn't just leave you with this bleak news. It offers some recommendations for transforming yourself and workplace culture. One specific recommendation that resonated with me is to change your workplace from a culture of paycheck to a culture of purpose. This report is spot on and aligns very closely with what I see as the starting points for cultivating an attitude that enjoys, promotes and sustains the Agile Principles.

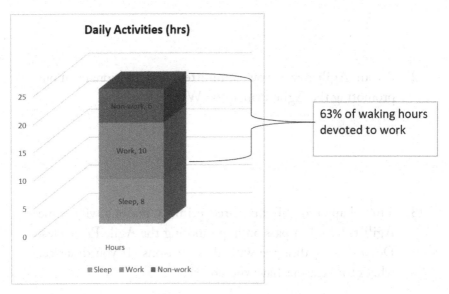

Figure 4: Daily Activities

Introduction - Study Questions

1. Gallup categorized the employees in the American workforce as either *engaged*, *disengaged* or *not engaged*. Based on the descriptions of each, which category do you fall in? Which category do the individuals on your team fall in?

2. As an Agilist, are you committed and passionate about promoting the Agile Principles? Why?

3. This chapter highlights three primary reasons why some Agilists have lost passion in promoting the Agile Principles. Do you agree/disagree with these reasons? If you disagree, what other reasons have you observed?

4. How many of your waking hours are devoted to your job? Do you hope to lessen, increase or are you satisfied with that number? Why?

1

Purpose of an Agilist

You may ask, what does purpose have to do with cultivating the right attitude to enjoy and promote the Agile Principles? To answer this question, I drew from the insight of Dr. Myles Munroe. Dr. Munroe wrote a book titled *The Spirit of Leadership*, and in his book, he stated: "Leadership is the capacity to influence others through inspiration motivated by a passion, generated by a vision, produced by a conviction, ignited by a purpose."[3] I believe this definition of leadership applies specifically also to an Agilist, who in many cases is the Agile supporter/enthusiast on the team.

This definition of leadership, I believe, gives us insight as to how we can generate the right attitude that will enable us to not only enjoy, but also to promote and sustain the Agile Principles. There are several different characteristics described in this definition:

- Purpose *will ignite conviction.*
- Conviction *will produce a vision.*
- Vision *will generate passion.*
- Passion *will motivate inspiration.*
- Inspiration *will lead to influence.*

The first characteristic, purpose, is what drives you. Purpose will prompt you to get up on a Monday morning with a smile on your face ready to attack the day. When a person identifies and is committed to a purpose, this allows them to "defy opposition, adversity, failure, disappointment, and discouragement."[4] We read about many historical figures who were so committed to a purpose that their degree of commitment fueled and sustained them to remain on the path even when they didn't feel like it. I appreciate Dr. Monroe's comments, "When a person discovers a sense of purpose, it produces a passion for pursuing it and that passion is what inspires other people to want to join in that pursuit."[5] We see examples of purpose-driven passion from individuals such as Nelson Mandela and Sir Winston Churchill.

Nelson Mandela functioned passionately with a purpose of ending legal discrimination (apartheid) in South Africa and fought to establish equal rights and opportunity for all. Even after spending 27 years in prison for allegedly conspiring to overthrow the state, he never lost sight of his purpose. This purpose drove and fueled him; this passion for his purpose eventually resulted in him becoming the first black president of South Africa. During his presidency, he focused on national reconciliation, worked tirelessly to ensure that the physiological needs of South Africa's poor were being provided for, and established many organizations to promote equality and fight AIDS. Another purpose-driven leader was Sir Winston Churchill. He was passionate about establishing individual freedoms through parliamentary democracy and believed that it was worth fighting for. He demonstrated strong leadership against the Nazis; maintained high expectations for British soldiers during the war; and he wisely engaged and partnered with the United States to ultimately defeat their common enemies. Churchill's purpose "produced a tireless passion to prevail, and his confident, cheerful manner and powerful speeches are credited with keeping the morale of the English people ... Churchill's vision for Great Britain and the world influenced both individuals and nations to extend themselves beyond what they thought they were capable of to achieve victory."[6]

Both Mandela and Churchill made immeasurable contributions to their generation and beyond. Their efforts and legacies have left a lasting mark on human history. There are some key principles one can extract from these historical figures that can benefit us in our jobs. Mandela and Churchill's lives undoubtedly highlight the importance and implications of operating with a sense of purpose. As we see, purpose drives passion. Purpose provides an assignment and signals a sense of significance. Dr. Munroe comments, "You're pursuing something that gives your life meaning ... if you become distracted or opposition stands in your way, you'll still be pulled in the direction of your desire because you can't imagine not fulfilling it."[7]

But what specifically does the concept of purpose have to do with that of the Agilist? Agilists of the world have a purpose of thoroughly understanding, appreciating and embracing the principles of Agile. Failing to see this as part of your purpose will limit your effectiveness in carrying out the principles on a day to day basis. Below are the examples of behaviors of an Agilist (i.e. Scrum Master) who has embraced this purpose.

- An Agilist who truly believes in the Agile Principles (i.e. #1 Satisfying customer with valuable software), will make every effort to ensure that his or her team is adhering to practices (i.e. Definition of Done, Definition of Ready) that will increase the likelihood for the team to deliver valuable software.
- An Agilist who truly believes in the Agile Principles (i.e. #11 Self-organizing teams create the best requirements, design and architecture) will always respectfully confront

the opinionated and contentious team member that is putting the team's ability to self-organize at risk.

- An Agilist who truly believes in the Agile Principles (i.e. #4 Business people and development team work together daily) will always explain to the Product Owner the need for her to be accessible to the development team.

I firmly believe that when we see that our purpose as an Agilist is to (1) thoroughly understand appreciate and embrace the Agile Principles and (2) thoroughly understand, appreciate and embrace the mission of your organization, this will cause us to have a different perspective on our jobs. When you understand the correlation between the application of Agile Principles and potential business growth of your company, there's a strong likelihood that passion will ensue. When you see that your role as an Agilist in the company is not minimal or passive but is essential for company growth, a new level of excitement will emerge. Business growth does not happen by accident. Varying levels of the organization have a responsibility of seeing customer satisfaction as a critical focus and doing everything they can to accomplish this. It's no surprise that satisfying customers with valuable software is the first Agile principle. We want to satisfy customers with valuable software to ensure customer retention and business growth. As discussed earlier, not every team member will be engaged, and not every team member will see the importance of this goal. This is where employing the Definition of Done (DoD) can be a very helpful technique for establishing and maintaining a quality-driven approach. In my experience, most teams have not welcomed this approach with open arms. Some will make statements such as "we should already know and remember to do these things; we don't need a checklist." A valid point, but my experience unfortunately tells me that most will forget to do some of the fundamental planning and design activities if not prompted.

I can think of one developer who fought daily against this technique and encouraged other developers to do the same. It almost seemed as though he wanted to turn everyone against me. I'm glad to say it didn't work. I know that DoD works. Given that the team wasn't diligent in adhering to the DoD, our team certainly paid the price in constant rework due to lack of code review and insufficient testing before merging the code to the appropriate branch. I took the opportunity to bring this up in the retrospective and in this case, the resistant developer was one of the culprits. The look on his face when he saw the consequences of his actions was priceless. He finally got it. To reinforce this learning, I reminded him every now and then about the incident. He started to see why I was making a big deal out of something he perceived to be ignorable. The big issues we oftentimes observe in our projects can be attributed to neglect in doing the small things we're supposed to do.

In my environment, we anticipate that requirements and priorities are going to change as we uncover more details about the strategic initiatives. With the understanding that progressive elaboration will occur, the Agilist doesn't have to be anxious or shaken. Unfortunately, the opposite can happen. You see, the Agilist doesn't ignore the challenges; she sees them. However, she's simultaneously choosing to look beyond them as she's guided and committed to the purpose (i.e. understanding, appreciating and embracing the mission of the organization). This commitment can provide calmness and contentment. Dr. Munroe points out, "[…] purpose sustains contentment. It supports a tranquility that refuses to be ruffled by the changing circumstances and states that pass through our lives."[8]

I recall during a Scrum of Scrum our team was informed by product management that the scope of the current release would be changed due in large part to a regulatory change in the industry.

Keep in mind, the teams had already gone through hours upon hours of planning for the release, so it was not surprising that several members of the team were not supportive of this change. I get it. We conducted grooming session after grooming session only to find out that the scope was changing. To be honest, I was disappointed as well. After the immediate shock, I was jolted back to the principles, specifically the principle of welcoming changes to requirements (Agile Principle #2). I needed to take the focus off myself and the inconvenience this would cause to me, and begin to ask a series of questions centered on understanding how this would benefit the organization and our customers. When that focus shifted, the anxiety that sometimes accompanies unplanned changes began to subside.

A Scrum Master for one of the teams who was visibly upset with this change became very combative with the product management team. She was one of my direct reports. When I noticed this behavior, I respectfully asked her to lower her voice and requested that she and I speak later. In our follow up conversation, I asked her the following:

- Do you understand what prompted the regulatory change?
- Do you understand how this will impact the organization?

She answered "no" to both questions. I suggested to her that in those moments she be intentional in suppressing the initial anger and frustration, assume no ill intentions of the messenger, and seek to genuinely understand the rationale of the change — specifically the impact to our organization and its respective customers. She appreciated the feedback and expressed that she would do better next time.

Ultimately, operating with this sense of purpose gives confidence. You have confidence because you are assured that your commitment to this purpose will put you on the right course, whether it's correcting a colleague or even advocating for unpopular practices that will undoubtedly incur resistance. Although each day will look different, your rationale for why you're doing what you're doing is filled with clarity and intentionality. With purpose as your guide, you'll move with objectivity and contentment. Objectivity is now possible because when you come to work each day your perspective extends beyond the everyday challenges and keeps you grounded and focused.

Purpose of an Agilist - Study Questions

1. What purpose was Nelson Mandela committed to? What were some of the challenges he encountered in his commitment to this purpose?

2. What is the purpose/mission of your company?

3. What is your role in helping the organization meet its mission? Do you see your role as valuable? If not, why?

4. Explain in your own words the purpose and benefits of each the Agile Principles.

5. Is your organization or team applying any of the Agile Principles? If so, which ones? Are there any steps they need to take to maintain commitment to these principles?

6. If you answered no to the previous question, do you think your company can benefit by starting to adopt these principles? If so, what initial steps would you suggest?

2

Conviction of an Agilist

The understanding, appreciation and embracing of your purpose will ignite a conviction. Conviction is necessary for an Agilist. It is defined as a fixed or firm belief and is a critical attribute in the pursuit of enjoying, sustaining and promoting the Agile Principles. You can't fake conviction; either you have it, or you don't. The degree of conviction you have is dependent on how much you trust the purpose, as the purpose "when captured, ignites a conviction."[9] A lack of conviction may be due to a lack of understanding or commitment to the purpose. Without conviction, we easily falter amid opposition. Therefore, it is essential that an Agilist maintain a strong conviction to their purpose in anticipation to the likely opposition they'll experience. When I think about conviction, one colleague comes to mind. In writing this book, I asked her, "What makes you continue to passionately execute your responsibilities despite the challenges and difficulties?" I worked with this colleague for over a year and have witnessed strong convictions from her. In response to my question, I heard the following comments from my colleague as it pertains to her role in helping the company meet its goals:

- "I know we can do it (get the job done). I'm looking at it positively and putting my business hat on."

- "This is my job, and I am determined to get us where we need to go."
- "This is not an impossible target."
- "I have a responsibility."

These comments reveal the inner motivation of my colleague. She understood the purpose of the business and her role, and held strong convictions for passionately carrying out her responsibilities in helping the company meet its objectives.

One historical figure who exemplified conviction is the Apostle Paul. He was one of the chief missionaries of early Christianity. Once a persecutor of Christians, Paul underwent a radical transformation and became one of the great characters in the Bible. He eventually went on to lead three fruitful missionary journeys. These journeys didn't come without some challenges. It was during these challenges his convictions emerged. Here Paul describes some of the challenges he experienced, captured in the New International Version Bible:

> I have worked much harder, been in prison more frequently, been flogged more severely, and been exposed to death again and again. Five times I received from the Jews the forty lashes minus one. Three times I was beaten with rods, once I was pelted with stones, three times I was shipwrecked, I spent a night and a day in the open sea, I have been constantly on the move. I have been in danger from rivers, in danger from bandits, in danger from my fellow Jews, in danger from Gentiles; in danger in the city, in danger in the country, in danger at sea; and in danger from false believers. I have labored and toiled and have often gone without sleep; I have known hunger and

thirst and have often gone without food; I have
been cold and naked.[10] (2 Cor. 11:23-27)

Despite all Paul's trials, there is no evidence he wavered in his
convictions. His commitment to his purpose of preaching the
Gospel to non-Jews ignited a conviction that was unceasing.

A lack of conviction can be a huge detriment to any organization
or long-term effort. The financial crisis of Fiat during the mid-
1990s serves as an example of what can happen when there's a
lack of conviction among the company's key decision makers.
In the late 80s and early 90s, Fiat was experiencing tremendous
success, as they accounted for more than 50% of the market share
of Italy's auto business. After these golden years, the organization
entered a rough financial season. Robert Herbold summarizes
the challenges Fiat faced. They were "suffering from excessive
executive turnover, stifling bureaucracy, and unexciting cars ...
tough decisions were not being made, and as a result, a company
that was once a national treasure was being run into the ground."[11]

This was nothing short of a catastrophe. By mid-2004, the
company had incurred more than $12 billion in losses over 5
years. Then came a leader with conviction. Sergio Marchionne
was hired as the new CEO of Fiat in June 2004. When he joined
the company, he fired Fiat managers that weren't contributing to
his vision. He brought in new talent, and maintained the existing
talent that dreamed big and had high energy. Marchionne also
led the innovation of new models, the remake of existing models,
and eliminated initiatives that were not having an impact. They
experienced years of increasing sales due to these efforts. The
conviction and courage to carry out these initiatives were fueled
by his purpose to see Fiat reclaim its previous glory. Without this
conviction, Marchionne would've likely failed to make the tough
decisions like his predecessors. As a result of his commitment to

the purpose, "Fiat returned to profitability for the first time since 2000. Revenues reached $31.1 billion, up 35 percent from 2005. Trading profits moved from a loss of $332 million in 2005 to a profit of $384 million in 2006. The Fiat Group announced that in 2007 it would pay its first dividend in five years."[12]

Do you have conviction? If not, I would encourage you to dig deep and begin nurturing that quality. A sense of conviction is the belief that's going to cause you to stand up for the right things and stand against the wrong. The effectiveness of the Agilist is proportionate to his or her strongly held beliefs. Conviction is ignited by the purpose and can be nurtured by internal faithfulness and consistent wisdom.[13] You'll need conviction to be a successful change agent for your team and organization. This is not just a cliché. Do you want to be a catalyst to nudge your organization in the right direction? I asked myself this question during an organization initiative to drive our teams to continuous delivery and deployment. When I first heard about the initiative, I was a little intimidated due to my limited understanding of the concepts. As I learned more about the initiative, I realized that the success of this effort would enable the teams to deliver working software more frequently. This is Agile Principle #3. Developing this ability would allow the teams to get feedback early and often to ensure we're building in accordance with the expectations, wants and needs of the customer. This effort was also a push towards technical excellence (Agile Principle #9), which in turn would help to promote a more sustainable pace (Agile Principle #8).

Understanding the implications of this effort, compelled me to grow in my understanding of the concepts. I went ahead and purchased a credible resource to help me get up to speed. I had a strong desire for the teams to improve. At this point, we weren't in the position to have new, fully tested, working software readily available for customers. I wanted us to get quick feedback on the health of our builds and a more repeatable and reliable build process. The long nights and weekends to get a high-quality build out to our customers were starting to take its toll. Morale was very low. I remember a few times working on the weekends and getting the not so nice looks from my wife.

To make these improvements, our team worked closely with a consultant to select the appropriate configuration management tool. I worked closely with the consultant and our team to develop a migration plan to transfer our customers' staging and production environments onto newly managed virtual machines so that we would have the infrastructure to deliver software more seamlessly and frequently. We witnessed amazing improvements. One of the technical leads involved in the process described some of the specific improvements:

> It [the new infrastructure] has allowed us to standardize our QX (staging and production setup) and configuration files in a way that allows us to deploy with confidence the same set of files across multiple servers. For example, for jboss, we are looking at over 120 jboss instances having the exact same set-up process. It also allows us to ensure we are deploying dependent systems like splunk and apache web servers in a seamless manner. The fact that the configurations are all stored and deployed from a master server improves the maintenance as well as providing and audit trail of who did what.

These changes led to improved morale. And although this was a challenging experience, it was an encouraging reminder that positive changes will require conviction. Conviction in some instances will prompt you to acknowledge your limitations while simultaneously motivating you to equip yourself to get the appropriate knowledge and skillset to drive that change.

Conviction of an Agilist - Study Questions

1. Do you possess conviction for the mission of your organization? Why?

2. Do you possess conviction for the Agile Principles? Why?

3. If you answered "no" to any of these questions, what are some steps you can take to nurture that conviction?

4. What was the Apostle Paul's purpose? What were some of the challenges he faced in his commitment to his purpose?

5. Sergio Marchionne operated with strong convictions. As a result, he made some very tough decisions for the betterment of the organization. Are there changes you would like to make to your organization? If so, have you started the process? If not, what prevents you from doing so?

3

Vision of an Agilist

Conviction will produce a vision. Standing firm in what you believe in will prompt you to start assessing whether the current state of things in the organization/team is aligned with your conviction. In cases when they aren't, you start to daydream. You envision a new reality; you see a roadmap; you begin to consistently visualize an improved and efficient way of how things can eventually be executed in the organization. You start to tell yourself that things in the organization can be better. You begin thinking about it more and more. You begin to think about the initial steps we need to take. Vision is essential. There's a saying "where there is no vision, the people are unrestrained..."[14]. Essentially, when there is no clear vision or objective that you're pursuing you tend to become susceptible to embracing many activities that are void of any meaning or significance. On the other hand, having a vision prompts a person to have a very focused life. Having a vision helps one to have self-discipline. In his book, *7 Habits of Highly Effective People,* Stephen Covey expounds on this topic when he suggests that we 'Begin with the end in mind.' This way of thinking will cause you to define, maintain and effectively contribute to the vision. Covey talks more about the value of vision stating that "to begin with the end in mind means to start with a clear understanding of your destination. It means to know

27

where you're going so that you better understand where you are now so that the steps you take are always in the right direction."[15] As you see, it is essential to have a vision of what you want to accomplish in either your organization, team or yourself; and the commitment to that vision will function as the fuel you need to keep progressing towards that goal. Unfortunately, not everyone will see the value in either creating a vision or maintaining a commitment to a vision. In *Developing the Leader Within You Workbook,* John Maxwell speaks about the four vision levels of people:

1. Some people never see it (they are wanderers).
2. Some people see it but never pursue it on their own (they are followers).
3. Some people see it and pursue it (they are achievers).
4. Some people see it and pursue it and help others see it (they are leaders).[16]

I believe Agilists should always function at the fourth level and have an unclouded vision for themselves, their teams, and their organizations. As an Agilist, having a vision helps you to choose clear priorities: choose what you read, choose your to do list, choose your attitude toward work, people and challenges. The Agilist should at least have a purpose of thoroughly understanding, appreciating and embracing the Agile Principles and the mission of the organization. That purpose should be the core and fuel of whatever vision you construct. This is at the core of how I function as an Agilist, thereby heavily influencing the vision that I have for myself, team and organization when I come to work each day. Each of the 12 Agile Principles, when reviewed closely, tend to fall into the categories of either customer satisfaction, quality, teamwork or project management. The commitment to these principles, my organization and personal convictions combine to represent the vision I have when I come into work each day.

```
                        Vision of an Agilist

Personal Convictions
    •   I will work with all my heart as though I'm working for God and not man.
    •   I will treat all colleagues with respect and dignity, seeing them as people made in the image of God.
    •   I will commit to maintaining an understanding and appreciation of my organization's strategic vision,
        portfolio, and projects.

Customer Satisfaction
    •   I will see customer satisfaction as a critical focus for the team and organization.
    •   I will work closely with teams to help them understand the importance of customer satisfaction and their
        role in helping to achieve this.

Quality
    •   I will commit to producing quality in every work that we ship.
    •   I will challenge every team member to produce his or her best work.

Teamwork
    •   I will strongly value team cooperation, team building, motivated team members and empowered team
        members.
    •   I will work closely and passionately with teams to promote unity and empowerment.

Project Management
    •   I will maintain an unwavering focus in keeping the teams work and progress clear and accessible to all.
    •   I will value team members involvement in near and long-term planning.
    •   I will help team members understand the significance of their role in the overall planning and execution of
        work.
```

Figure 5: My Vision as an Agilist

This vision keeps me focused. If I'm ever uncertain of what to work on next at my job I can always look to this vision for guidance. Pursuit of a vision will always present some challenges. As you ponder your vision and begin your pursuit of it, ask yourself the following questions:

- What do others see?
- Why do they see it that way?
- How can I change their perception?

These questions are crucial in helping to construct a roadmap for navigating through the challenges and achieving the vision. This came into play during my time as a Scrum Master. I was the Scrum Master for two software development teams that were working on the same product. Both teams were working on key features that would be a part of an upcoming major release. Some of the key challenges with these teams were: (1) the development team for each team were neither aligned nor clear on the sprint goals of the other team (2) the development team wasn't clear on the overall progress of the release (3) many team members were neither motivated nor collaborative and (4) there was a poorly defined release management process.

My vision was to introduce project management and teamwork practices that team members would value and thereby take ownership of and maintain them. In my effort to do this, I needed to objectively assess the situation, specifically (1) What do others see? (2) Why do they see it that way? (3) How can I change their perception?

- What do others see?
  - A small group saw the problems as I did and was frustrated.
  - Another group saw the problems, was indifferent to them and didn't feel compelled to do anything about them, given that the problems had been around for so long.

- Why do they see it that way?
  - One group believed the teams could do better but felt they needed more support from management.
  - The second group seemed to just not care.

- How can I change their perception?
  - Clearly explain the adverse impact if the problems remain unaddressed (using visuals and charts).
  - Have one on one sessions with the influencers of the team and urgently express to them that they can be the catalyst for making positive changes to the team. Most of these people were achievers ("achievers" are defined as those that see the vision and pursue it). My

goal was to empower them to be leaders that see the vision, pursue it, and help others see it.

Ultimately, due to a combined effort between the achievers and myself, the teams were successful in overcoming their differences. Most of the team members began operating in a mission-conscious and collaborative manner enabling them to meet the schedule and scope objectives.

As seen in the vision above, I strongly value team cooperation, team building, motivated team members and empowered team members. When I think about these components, several thoughts come to mind. One idea is the cooperation between the developers of the product and the customer (or a representative of the customer who understands the expectations of the customer). In most cases, this person is typically identified as the product owner. This relationship is vital and can be costly to the organization if not managed appropriately. Without a good handle on this, you can spend sprint after sprint building the wrong thing. My team and I experienced this, and I promise it was not pretty. We worked with the product owner (or the person with the title) for 10 sprints believing we were on the right track. At the sprint 10 review, the product owner's boss attended and made some very condescending remarks stating that we wasted the organization's money and built the wrong thing. This absolutely killed the team's morale. There are certain incidents in your career that you don't forget, and this is one of them for me.

The product owner we worked with for five months periodically attended our daily standups and consistently attended all sprint planning, review and grooming sessions. Given his attendance, there was no reason for the team to believe that we weren't building the right product. This miscommunication was costly. Significant rework needed to occur in order for the product to reach an acceptable state. This experience, while a loss in many aspects was a major lesson learned for me that these roles are critical and require individuals that are committed. In retrospect, I realize that this product owner didn't fully understand his responsibilities. Although he participated in training courses this doesn't always translate into a motivated and equipped product owner. I also think of what I could've done differently. I could've devoted more time reinforcing the fundamentals of the product owner role and reminded him that he needed to be more readily available and empowered to represent client and stakeholder interests.

These moments in your career will reinforce the need to hold firmly to specific principles. They will ultimately highlight the need for you to establish a vision that will enable you to operate with consistency, become a constant voice of reason within your organization and help you avoid costly mistakes.

Vision of an Agilist - Study Questions

1. John Maxwell talks about the four vision levels of people. Do you agree or disagree that the Agilist should function at the fourth level? Why?

2. I created a vision for myself that centered around my personal convictions, the organization's mission, and the Agile Principles. Do you have a vision for yourself? If yes, have you begun executing the vision? If not, why?

3. If you haven't yet created a vision – do you see the value of creating one? Why?

4

Passion of an Agilist

When influencers on a team are bought into the vision, this will lead to a passionate pursuit to seeing this vision realized. This passion will translate into a sense of obligation and deep commitment. An Agilist should function with the same obligation and deep commitment. Visualizing how things can be, recognizing that the circumstances do not have to remain as is, and wanting to see that new reality will drive the Agilist. Some Agilists are interested in carrying out the 12 principles but are not *committed*. The Agilists operating with a sense of purpose, conviction, and vision are not merely interested, they are *committed*. As Munroe points out, "Commitment is the guy who jumps out of an airplane, trusting that the parachute will open. It's not talk, but action. Passion makes you jump in, no matter what. Leaders are committed, not just interested. They are willing to put their whole selves into accomplishing their purposes."[17]

The Agilist may be content, but should never be satisfied until the vision is achieved. They should maintain a knowledge of and appetite for what's next. To nurture this passion, I schedule time every week for myself to memorize, meditate and reflect on my organization's mission and the culture we're hoping to achieve. By doing this I'm feeding my passion, otherwise I risk developing habits of laziness, stagnancy and ineptitude. I spend too much time at the office to develop those habits. I have to resist them. If you don't nurture your passion, don't be surprised to see it lessen. As an Agilist it becomes increasingly challenging to inspire and lead others if you're not passionate yourself. In *H3 Leadership*, Brad Lomenick highlights the significance of passion and the critical role it plays in a leader's life, "Your team feeds off your energy, for better or worse. Your passion gives permission to those around you to express theirs. You may have to push, pull, kick, or gently nudge people but part of your responsibility as a leader is to show up, every day, with a level of energy, passion and enthusiasm that elevates your attitude toward constant positivity. You don't have a choice. Leaders are organizational risks or assets. You've got to love it and live it if you're going to lead it."[18]

The motto I repeat to myself and what helps me to keep my foot on the pedal is to *live as though I'll die tomorrow and pursue the vision for the sake of a better tomorrow*. It doesn't matter if others are not operating with your level of intensity. As a matter of fact, don't be surprised if they're not. Don't let that discourage you. Instead, pull them up to your level of passion, don't let them pull you down.

Remain passionate about the Agile Principles even when others aren't. While the concepts and benefits of the principles are clear, applying it can be very challenging. Take for example Agile Principle #6, which promotes face-to-face conversations, as it allows for the quickest transfer of information between parties. Most are aware that face to face is the most efficient means of communication, however, for someone with social anxiety disorder, a simple conversation can become a very arduous task. Individuals with social anxiety are fearful that they will be humiliated, judged and rejected. These individuals not only have a hard time updating their team during the daily standups, but they have a hard time with just going to work and doing everyday things. Below are some additional symptoms of social anxiety:

- Show a rigid body posture, make little eye contact, or speak with an overly soft voice
- Find it scary and difficult to be with other people, especially those they don't already know, and have a hard time talking to them even though they wish they could
- Are very self-conscious in front of other people and feel embarrassed and awkward
- Are very afraid that other people will judge them[19]

I've been around colleagues with social anxiety, and my heart goes out to them. Whether I'm in the role of a Scrum Master or Project Manager, I feel an obligation to ensure that members on the team with this anxiety recognize that they're integral to the team and that they have a voice. With one gentleman, I recall in our one on one how candid he was about his anxiety. I probed a little to find out what specific factors would trigger his anxiety. He explained that his experience in the organization had mostly been unpleasant, specifically with the managers and technical leads. Gaining additional context around the factors that contributed to his anxiety was a big deal. Armed with this information, I would cautiously approach him when I needed to give him feedback and would always remind him that I wanted to see him succeed. Additionally, I would pay close attention to the team dynamics to observe how other team members were treating him. I've built a great rapport with him and have seen improvements in how he's setting boundaries and expectations with team members to better manage his anxiety.

Human relationships can be messy sometimes. In some cases, the root cause is poor communication. People just don't listen to each other sometimes — especially when its face to face. Ian

Tuhovsky remarks, "Unfortunately, too many of us don't actually listen to our conversation partner in the hope of understanding them. In fact, we tend to listen just so we know when we can next take our own place in the spotlight without appearing too rude!"[20] These aren't conversations. There's no exchange of information for mutual benefit and enjoyment; it becomes a silly game of when do I get to speak next.

My perspective on face-to-face conversation has radically shifted in the past few years. I now view people differently. This perspective has improved the productivity of my conversations. It all started after I read the story of the Good Samaritan:

> On one occasion an expert in the law stood up to test Jesus. "Teacher," he asked, "what must I do to inherit eternal life?" "What is written in the Law?" he replied. "How do you read it?"
>
> He answered: "'Love the Lord your God with all your heart and with all your soul and with all your strength and with all your mind'; and, 'Love your neighbor as yourself.'" "You have answered correctly," Jesus replied. "Do this and you will live."
>
> But he wanted to justify himself, so he asked Jesus, "And who is my neighbor?"
>
> In reply Jesus said: "A man was going down from Jerusalem to Jericho, when he fell into the hands of robbers. They stripped him of his clothes, beat him and went away, leaving him half dead. A priest happened to be going down the same road, and when he saw the man, he passed by on the

other side. So too, a Levite, when he came to the place and saw him, passed by on the other side. But a Samaritan, as he traveled, came where the man was; and when he saw him, he took pity on him. He went to him and bandaged his wounds, pouring on oil and wine. Then he put the man on his own donkey, took him to an inn and took care of him. The next day he took out two silver coins and gave them to the innkeeper. 'Look after him,' he said, 'and when I return, I will reimburse you for any extra expense you may have.'

"Which of these three do you think was a neighbor to the man who fell into the hands of robbers?" The expert in the law replied, "The one who had mercy on him."

Jesus told him, "Go and do likewise." (Luke 10:25–37)[21]

The kindness of this Samaritan towards this half-dead Jew sheds light on the question 'Who is your neighbor?' and 'How do you treat your neighbor?' This story shows us that our neighbor is anyone who crosses our path, and our position towards them is to explore how we can meet their needs. The Samaritan treated this Jewish man as one would treat a family member. He placed his own activities on pause for the well-being of the Jewish man. Through this story, I've developed a better understanding of who my neighbor is. I now see my colleagues as my neighbors and as my family. I'm equipped by God to love them like family. I'm not fearful of their rejection because I am accepted by God; and I'm not yearning for their approval because I am approved by God. This mindset is so liberating. I'm less self-conscious and it puts me in a posture to better appreciate my colleagues, thereby making my face-to-face conversations more frequent and productive. Edward Welch clarifies the shift that happens to self-consciousness when we view others as family, "Now imagine for a moment. What would happen to your self-consciousness if you treated everyone as family? Usually, when you are home with family, you don't spend too much time thinking about their opinions of you. You aren't worried about your hair, weight, successes or failures. They might drive you crazy sometimes, but you deal with it. You have to. They are family."[22]

Establishing the right mindset is the first step in improving our face-to-face exchanges. Another factor to consider is our listening skills. There are several different listening positions one can take when engaging in face-to-face conversations. They can include the following:

- Critical – analyzing the facts behind a situation
- Empathetic – honoring feelings over bare facts … being present and paying attention
- Reductive – hoping they'll get to the most important points as quickly as possible
- Expansive – sitting patiently with the speaker as they work through their thoughts and feelings
- Active – consciously making an effort to understand what the other person is saying and reacting in an encouraging manner
- Passive – taking some of the information in, but not being too bothered if you don't hear or fully understand it[23]

In one incident, I went from being a critical listener to an empathetic listener. Let me explain. The person I needed to speak to had a potty mouth. He didn't start off that way, but after a few months on the job he began using offensive language during our meetings. Colleagues would gossip behind his back, but it didn't appear as though anyone wanted to confront him, including myself. However, after reaching my threshold, I realized I needed to say something. I didn't feel like it, but I needed to. I prayed about it, and felt convinced that I needed to make him aware that his language was starting to negatively impact the morale of the team. I sat nervously in the conference room waiting for him to join our one on one. As he walked in, his body language looked very defeated; as though he didn't want to be at the job anymore. Before I could get a word out, he unloaded on me. He explained the different bouts of anxiety and stress that he was facing. As I looked at him and carefully weighed his words and tone, my heart went out to him. Our conversation flowed effortlessly as he realized I was listening and had a genuine concern for his well-being. We briefly discussed his behavior, but not as much as I thought we would. The majority of the time was spent encouraging him to remain hopeful. What's interesting is that after our talk, I don't remember hearing any more offensive language from my colleague. I bring up this event to highlight the flexibility we should consider in our face to face interactions. Always assess the situation to determine which listening posture is ideal for the moment.

When the Agilist fully understands and embraces the purpose and benefits of Agile and the purpose and benefits of their organization, there's a strong likelihood that passion for their work will follow. They will become intentional and passionate in carrying out the principles of Agile so that it is directly supporting the achievement of the organization's vision. This passion will sometimes translate into initiating that potentially awkward conversation that may require candidness and vulnerability on your end. A byproduct of your effort is that others in the organization will witness the credibility of Agile and the role it plays in helping the company to meet its goals.

Passion of an Agilist - Study Questions

1. Are you passionate about the mission of your organization? Why?

2. Are you passionate about the Agile Principles? Why?

3. If you answered "no" to any of the first two questions, what steps can you take to nurture that passion?

4. Explain why following this motto can help to nurture a sense of urgency and passion: *"Live as though I'll die tomorrow and pursue the vision for the sake of a better tomorrow."*

5. Do you think the idea of viewing your colleagues as family members can help improve your face-to-face interactions? Why?

5

The Inspiring Agilist

As I think about some of the best leaders I've followed, the common attribute I observed was passion. That passion was attractive, it was appealing, it was motivating, and it was inspiring. The energy and excitement they displayed were mentally stimulating and would compel me to stop what I was doing so I could understand what made them behave this way. Once they got my attention through their passion, I could better understand their vision, see the intensity of their conviction, see the rationale behind their purpose, and develop an appreciation for that purpose.

The term inspire means to "fill someone with the urge or ability to do or feel something, especially to do something creative."[24] As an Agilist, possessing the ability to inspire is key. It can't be fake. That inspiration is likely to be borne out of the following: (1) understanding the purpose/benefits of Agile and its ability to help your organization meet its goals (2) that purpose igniting a conviction (3) that conviction producing a vision to see things operate in a more efficient manner via Agile Principles (4) that vision generating a passion to see that envisioned reality come to life (5) that passion will then motivate inspiration. You see, that ability to inspire comes from within, and it starts first with the recognition and appreciation of the purpose of your role as an

Agilist and your appreciation for the purpose of the organization that you support.

The ability to inspire will determine the success of the Agilist in her organization. Motivating people to function with an Agile mindset is a very challenging task. You're literally asking them in some cases to abandon some of the ways they've been doing things for a very long time. You're asking them to enter the unknown. Many people tend to be fearful of new things and more often than not, people are resistant to change. The Harvard Business Review does a great job of succinctly capturing 10 reasons why people are resistant to change. They include:

1. Loss of control: *Change interferes with autonomy and can make people feel that they've lost control over their territory.*
2. Excess uncertainty: *If change feels like walking off a cliff blindfolded, then people will reject it.*
3. Surprise, surprise!: *Decisions imposed on people suddenly, with no time to get used to the idea or prepare for the consequences, are generally resisted.*
4. Everything seems different: *Routines become automatic, but change jolts us into consciousness, sometimes in uncomfortable ways.*
5. Loss of face: *When change involves a big shift of strategic direction, the people responsible for the previous direction dread the perception that they must have been wrong.*
6. Concerns about competence: *Change is resisted when it makes people feel stupid.*
7. More work: *Here is a universal challenge. Change is indeed more work.*
8. Ripple effects: *Like tossing a pebble into a pond, change creates ripples, reaching distant spots in ever-widening circles.*

9. Past resentments: *The ghosts of the past are always lying in wait to haunt us. As long as everything is in a steady state, they remain out of sight.*

10. Sometimes the threat is real: *Change is resisted because it can hurt. When new technologies displace old ones, jobs can be lost; prices can be cut; investments can be wiped out.*[25]

Given that there's a strong likelihood of resistance, an Agilist must learn to lead well. You're taking people to a new place. Dr. Munroe captures it well, "True leadership fundamentally requires the responsibility of taking followers into the exciting unknown and creating a new reality for them."[26] If it's up to them, most people would gladly stay in the status quo and make comments such as "I like doing things the old way because I'm comfortable with it." You're getting ready to take them on an adventure — a potentially bumpy and emotional roller coaster ride. The Agilist is attempting to get people "stirred to participate in the positive vision that you are presenting them."[27]

As Agilists take their team into unfamiliar territory, some will choose to follow, others will resist and will even influence others to resist. I can think of several experiences where people were very reluctant to embrace certain Agile Principles. One person that comes to mind is Jane (not her real name). She was in product and part of her responsibilities was to convey and clarify the vision of the product to the team. Although she would say, "I'll give this Agile thing a shot," her actions would say otherwise. Jane's comments to the rest of the team discouraged them from becoming more self-organized and self-directing. I needed to understand why; I needed to understand the motivation behind her behavior. After a few one on ones with Jane, it became clear that the primary factor behind this behavior was a fear of the team not meeting their objectives and delivering the software on time. Realizing that fear was the driving factor, I needed to explore options for how I could begin to change her perception, otherwise she was going to continue being a strong hindrance to the team operating at their highest potential.

The first thing I did was to ask Jane questions to help her become aware of what was happening. My questions focused on occasions when her behavior disrupted the natural flow of the team. For example, during a sprint review when a developer gave a demo, one of the stakeholders had a question for the developer. Instead of allowing the developer to answer the question, Jane immediately jumped in, robbing the developer of the opportunity to answer the question. Worse yet, she communicated through her actions that she didn't think the developer was competent enough to answer the question. I followed up with Jane about this and explained to her that her behavior could inadvertently suppress the confidence and creativity of the developers. I explained to her the importance of her role and responsibilities in helping the team become more self-organized. I consistently reminded Jane that objective evidence affirms the eleventh Agile principle — self-organizing teams build the best requirements, design and architecture.

Jane was receptive to my feedback and confirmed that she would make a stronger effort to adjust her approach. I'm encouraged to say that I saw an improvement in Jane. There were some moments when she fell back to her old habits, but for the most part I witnessed someone acknowledging a need to change and a motivation to move in the right direction. Overall, I was very respectful, but mostly tried to let my passion about ensuring that the team operated in a self-organized manner show. I had a sense of obligation and deep commitment to the team. That passion was birthed from a vision that came from a desire to see the team functioning more purposefully in meeting the goals and objectives of the organization.

Another experience regarding resistance to change, involved my joining a new team. I was asked to help improve the process for the prioritization, visibility and execution of the work. For teams to operate in a way that efficiently welcomes change to requirements (Agile Principle #2) and promote a sustainable and constant pace (Agile Principle #8) they need to have in place a culture that communicates clearly and openly, with the team's work and progress clear and accessible to all. This new team communicated in a very destructive manner. I decided to dig deeper into the communication issues. As a new person to the team you're at a disadvantage because you don't have the context to know what's going on. However, you're also at an advantage because you're out of the loop and in a prime position to objectively assess, ask the tough questions, and give feedback to the team. The fact that these issues were lingering for so long indicated that the teams were not using the retrospectives effectively to identify and develop action plans for their concerns. Retrospectives shouldn't just be a formality. Agilists should see problems on the team as a stepping-stone, as an opportunity to prune away some of the inefficiencies in the effort to maintain or improve the health of the team. The retrospective sessions help to facilitate this. There are tons of resources out there to assist the Agilist in these sessions. Regardless of the tools or exercises one chooses to use, the Agilist needs to care. That's been one of the biggest takeaways for me. One should look at these sessions as a golden opportunity to really help the teams take one step in the right direction.

With this team, I decided to schedule a working agreement session, and, in that meeting, I passionately expressed to the team that they'd never become a high-performing team until they learned how to communicate openly and clearly to each other. Due to all the hostility between the team members, this meeting slowly transitioned into a retrospective. This clearly wasn't planned, but it was the right direction to take. I tried my best to stay calm, positive and objective. I quickly learned there was some bitterness, animosity, lack of trust, and a technical leader that was not equipped to be the leader (the team did not trust him; he needed training). I encouraged the manager of the technical leader to remove him from that role if we wanted to see the team improve. Surprisingly, it was a seamless and painless move. The technical leader was receptive to the move and expressed that he understood that this change was necessary to help improve the dynamics of the team. The team was eventually successful in constructing shared working agreements. In the process of doing this, I witnessed team members diligently pointing out behavior patterns they wanted the team to either stop doing or begin adopting (i.e. come to meetings on time, always have an agenda for meetings, give team members enough time to estimate their work).

Another area that I needed to address with this team was improving the visibility of the project's progress. The product manager had her own method for tracking and communicating progress, however, the process she used was tedious, unreliable and error prone. Shortly after seeing this process at work, I encouraged her to reconsider the process and explore another approach. She immediately told me that she was not changing her process. At that point, I had the option of either conceding to what she said or continuing to advocate the importance of fixing the problem. It's during these times, I rely on my purpose, which will fuel my conviction, produce a vision, and consequently generate passion. Remembering my purpose, I passionately reminded her that we have an obligation to improve how we were conveying information about the project's progress to stakeholders and team members. As with Jane's situation, I needed to understand the motivation behind this behavior and try to change her perception. After a few discussions it became clear why this product manager felt this way. She explained that someone previously attempted to "improve" the way she structured her project but failed to sufficiently instruct her on the specific changes that were made and how to efficiently manage the improved structure on her own. After a few one on ones, she began to understand that my motives were sincere, and she eventually became open to tweaking the process. Given my understanding of the circumstances, the product manager and I (1) brainstormed on a model that would work best for the type of work her team was doing (2) met three times a week, for four weeks, to tweak the model to align with her expectations, wants and needs (3) discussed the model with the team to get their buy-in and feedback. The team was excited as they longed for more structure in the overall prioritization, planning and execution of work. I'm encouraged to say that in a matter of two months the team was communicating more openly and managing their work more efficiently.

As I worked through the resistance in the examples given, it was critical for me to understand the individual's perception. Their perception of the circumstances was driving their emotional response. Dr. Robert Kellemen, in his book *Soul Physicians*, offers a basic formula for helping us to better understand the emotions of our colleagues:

$$\text{External Situation (ES)} + \text{Internal Perception (IP)} = \text{Emotional Response (ER)}[28].$$

Essentially, our External Situation plus our Internal Perception leads to our Emotional Response. In the example above, we observe the following:

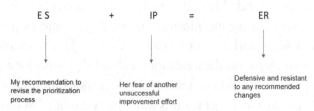

Figure 6: Internal Perception

This event further confirmed that once you understand the story behind the resistance, you'll be in a better position to respond.

Additionally, these experiences with resistance demonstrated to me that vision will generate passion and passion will motivate inspiration, which will then lead to influence. I've learned that the use of manipulation and intimidation to coerce others to follow your vision is not a sustainable approach. This is not effective leadership. Munroe sums it up well, "The fact is that true leadership is not control or manipulation of others, but it is other people's willful submission of their authority to yours, motivated by inspiration."[29] Agile leaders should inspire. They should function with the intent to influence others towards the adoption of the Agile Principles. They influence others through inspiration, motivated by a passion, generated by a vision, produced by a conviction, ignited by a purpose.

I've learned that it's essential to truly believe in what you're promoting. Otherwise, you may be deemed a hypocrite. I believe that the term Agile has unfortunately become both a buzz word and a nebulous term to many. If I'm in an elevator and I want to quickly describe Agile to someone, I would say "It's a set of principles aimed at governing how we view and address quality, teamwork, customer satisfaction, and project management with a desired outcome of improved employee and customer engagement." Those that are Agilists should bring clarity to this term and possess the ability to speak clearly on the purpose and benefits of these principles. It's beneficial for Agilists to become familiar with papers, case studies, etc. that highlight objective evidence of how well these principles are working. The benefit of this is that you're not just echoing what you've learned in a two-day course, but instead you're speaking with a sense of conviction and passion. The examples below highlight a few organizations and how they intentionally integrated these principles into the fabric of how they operate.

Example #1

A study of 438 organizations was conducted by the Aberdeen Group. These organizations were assessed/ranked based on data surrounding employee performance, employee engagement and employee retention. After the assessment, the organizations were grouped in the following categories:

- Best-in-Class (top 20%)
- Average (middle 50%)
- Laggard (bottom 30%)

I took note of the top 20%. These organizations (Best-in-Class) shared some common characteristics. They include:

- Senior leaders establish a culture of alignment and ongoing communication.
- Tools and practices that provide visibility and transparency into individual and organizational goals and progress.
- Full accountability among individuals and managers for business results.

These three characteristics are elements that organizations need to establish a framework of strong transparency, accountability and communication. This foundation will increase team accountability and responsibility. It's no surprise that these organizations were ranked in the top 20%. And it's primarily because they've recognized the value of employee engagement, and thereby made it a huge priority in how they operate. This type of mindset is consistent with the Agile Principles surrounding teamwork. The following Agile Principles reinforce team building, teamwork, and trust in self-managing teams:

- Principle #4: Business people and developers must work together daily throughout the project.
- Principle #5: Build projects around motivated individuals. Give them the environment and support they need and trust them to get the job done.
- Principle #6: The most efficient and effective method of conveying information to and within a development team is face-to-face conversation.
- Principle #8: Agile processes promote sustainable development. The sponsors, developers, and users should be able to maintain a constant pace indefinitely.
- Principle #11: The best architectures, requirements, and designs emerge from self-organizing teams.
- Principle #12: At regular intervals, the team then tunes and adjusts its behavior accordingly.

These principles, when applied passionately can have a positive and lasting impact. Like the Best-in-Class organizations, these principles can lead to improved employee performance, employee engagement and employee retention thereby increasing the likelihood for business growth.

Example #2

The RSA Global Digital teams identified concerns with the length of time it took to get their services to market. Additionally, they saw some inefficiencies in how work was being prioritized and executed. Specifically, they noted "operating in a mixed environment, completing planned work as well as responding to unplanned events had its challenges for the teams, who provide the front-end development and maintenance services for RSA web services."[30] The team saw the problems and realized that something had to be done. They employed Agile Principle #12

— At regular intervals the team reflects on how to become more effective, then tunes and adjusts its behavior accordingly.

To fine tune and adjust, the team brought everyone together to collectively walk through the end-to-end process and pinpoint areas of contention. The output of this session led to a common understanding of the problem areas and an improvement plan that centered around a training program to help achieve "a common understanding of current tools and terminology, plus tools to model the process and identify areas for future improvement."[31] This session led to several tangible outcomes for the teams:

- Motivation to adopt and develop better practices.
- A common understanding of terms, tools and processes to use and why (their value).
- A sense of ownership for ongoing improvement to processes adopted within the team.
- Greater visibility of work being undertaken and managed.
- Emphasis on, and ownership of, delivering quality products.

These improvements would in turn lead to an improved time to market. This session aimed at fine tuning and adjusting paid off exponentially.

Example 3

BBC iPlayer, an internet streaming catchup, television and radio service in the United Kingdom, was encountering problems with maintaining team cohesiveness and delivering services on very tight deadlines. To help get to the root of the problem, the team conducted a retrospective (Agile Principle #12). The outcome from the retrospective was that the team needed to improve their focus on delivering value to the audience. This is consistent with

Agile Principle #1 which states: Our highest priority is to satisfy the customer through early and continuous delivery of valuable software. Operating with this principle in mind helps to ensure customer retention and continuous business growth. Because of this focus, the team identified a list of the following action items that would allow them to be more customer focused.

- Establish a clearer vision and goals.
- Take the time to model their process; analyze and improve it.
- Reconsider and adapt roles.
- Take a fresh approach to dealing with dependencies and bugs.
- Reset their relationships with the Senior Leadership Team and take firmer control over agreeing to meet imposed deadlines.
- Improve their negotiation skills.

As a result of these changes, BBC iPlayer has experienced a 70% increase in demand for their services. Clearly the changes this company made have caught the attention of customers. Good for them!

Example #4

A two-year case study was conducted to highlight the qualitative and quantitative impact of introducing Scrum into an existing software development organization. Prior to the introduction of Scrum, this organization had ineffective planning meetings. Instead, they had weekly status meetings on Monday and impromptu status meetings with the president. Additionally, there was poor visibility into completed and planned work, a lack of process for managing rapidly changing requirements, and insufficient oversight on how work was distributed to the team.

Scrum is a lightweight Agile model with prescribed practices, roles, artifacts, events, and rules that reinforces the twelve principles. This model relies strongly on transparency, inspection and adaptation. With the implementation of Scrum, the team and organization experienced several improvements:

- Reduced Overtime:
  - The results of the case study showed that the percentage of overtime worked reduced from 19% to 7%. Given the details in the case, the reduction in overtime translates into the company saving $3,000 a week. One of the primary reasons for this was that the team was now operating at a more sustained pace.

- Satisfied Developers:
  - Developers confirmed that the introduction of Agile Principle #4 played a big part in their improvement, stating that the new practice "promotes better communication with the client ... it is useful to see customer representatives every day since there are always questions that could be asked" and "it makes me more confident in what we're doing because customers always have up-to-date information about the progress."[32]
  - Developers also acknowledged and praised the 7th and 12th principles, saying that the practices surrounding these principles were "useful, because not only can the customer see what we have achieved so far, but all the developers can see how it all works or doesn't work together."[33]

- Satisfied Customers:
  - Customers saw the value of the Agile Principles 2, 4, and 7. See some of their comments below confirming it:

- "The initiation of the Scrum process has led to our being more involved in the daily review and discussion. This has led to us being more aware and being held accountable earlier in the process for any changes or concerns that have or had to be considered."[34]

- "I have a greater respect for the software developers and understand how easy it is for expectations and results to differ without clear instruction and regular communication between all parties."

- When talking about the reviews, customers stated: "it has helped us as customers to visually see the product, and we are able to see them earlier in the process again. This has led to the ability to tweak and change the product in a timelier fashion. We as customers have found it difficult to visualize the product ahead of time, and some concerns have only arisen when the demonstrations have been shown."[35]

The Inspiring Agilist - Study Questions

1. Have you tried to inspire your team(s), but were met with resistance? If so, what was the reason for the resistance?

2. This chapter talked about the model, ES + IP = ER. In the resistance you encountered, what is the ES? IP? ER?

3. Looking back at that encounter is there anything you would've done differently?

4. Do you agree or disagree that understanding the internal perception (IP) of those that are resistant is essential for inspiring? Why?

5. Out of the four examples, which one best resembles your organization? Why? Do you think your organization can benefit from the same corrective action?

6. In example one, there are three common characteristics that the Best in Class organizations share. Does your organization thrive in any of these areas? If yes, what do you think are the primary reasons for this?

7. If you answered no to the questions above, which of these characteristics do you think your organization needs the most? What help can you provide to move them in this direction?

6

Driving Success in Your Organization via Agile

The primary encouragement throughout this book is for the Agilist to be driven by purpose to cultivate an attitude that enjoys, promotes and sustains the Agile Principles. Specifically, take ownership in growing in your understanding of the (1) purpose and benefits of your organization or projects and (2) purpose and benefits of each of the Agile Principles. When we understand, appreciate and embrace the purpose and benefits of the Agile Principles and see how the application of the principles directly support the mission of the organization and directly drives business growth, we'll cultivate a deeper passion for our job as an Agilist. Essentially, we will then make it our purpose to passionately carry out the principles of Agile so that it is directly supporting the achievement of the company's vision; and make it our purpose to passionately demonstrate to others in the organization how the execution of Agile Principles is helping the company to meet its goals. The diagram below attempts to capture the theme behind this book.

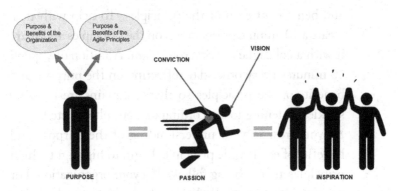

Figure 7: From Purpose to Inspiration

As mentioned, purpose ignites conviction; conviction produces vision; vision generates passion; passion motivates inspiration; and inspiration will lead to influence. The starting point is purpose. I would encourage the Agilist to try some of the following practices immediately to transition to a more purpose-driven mindset:

- Understand the purpose (or vision) of your company. Write out the purpose of the company in your own words and develop the ability to share this purpose with anyone at the drop of a dime.
- Understand the purpose of the projects you're working on. Understand the specific factors that are driving the project (i.e. fixing an existing issue, cost saving, addressing an external demand). Write out in your own words the purpose of the project and the description of the factors that are driving the project.
- Understand how the projects you're working on support the overall business strategy of your organization. Like the first two practices, write out in your own words how the project you're working on aligns with the business strategy.
- Become proficient in your understanding of the 12 Agile Principles. Develop the ability to clearly explain the purpose

and benefits of each of the principles. To help with this, create a 10-minute presentation on the principles and share it with a colleague or with your team. Additionally, spend 10 minutes every other day reflecting on the purpose and benefits of the principles so that it remains fresh (using stickies, listening to a recording on your phone, etc.).

• As you grow in your understanding of the purpose and benefits of each Agile principle, begin to highlight which principles are not being followed in your organization. For example, if you notice behaviors from team members that are contrary to a self-organizing team, be empowered to address that problem, as you now understand the negative impact of the team not operating consistently with Agile Principle #11 — the best architectures, requirements and design emerge from self-organizing teams. Appendix A is devoted to helping Agilists promote behaviors that will help push their teams to improve in responsibility and accountability, thereby functioning in a more self-organizing and self-directing manner.

As you begin to operate in a way that reflects these principles, anticipate that there may be some resistance to the practices that you implement or advocate. In those moments, hear the concerns and choose to empathize, but do not waiver or lose your passion in promoting these principles that will benefit your team, and ultimately your organization. There are going to be days when you may not feel like going to work, dealing with people, repeating yourself over and over, and mediating another conflict. In those moments, you'll need to encourage yourself. During those times of uncertainty, worry, frustration, and the feeling that the waves of life are shifting you back and forth and up and down, you need an anchor. You'll need something to keep you grounded that will be the fuel and motivation to begin the first step of pursuing that purpose. For me, that anchor is a love for God and a love for my neighbors. This is what gives me the zeal to learn and meditate on the purpose and benefits of the organization and the Agile Principles. This love drives me. This love causes me to courageously put aside my agenda. I get into the world of others, keep their well-being in mind, and potentially risk pain and rejection to provide them with hope and encouragement. I want what's best for my colleagues. This is the underpinning for my constant promotion and application of these principles with a desired outcome of a successful organization. If I can help my organization thrive, I'm helping my colleagues.

Appendix A: In Pursuit of Self-Organization via Scrum

When you read the Scrum Guide you see that the "rules of Scrum bind together specific roles, events and artifacts governing the relationships and interaction between them." [36] Regarding roles, Scrum prescribes a Product Owner, Scrum Master and Development Team. These roles make up the official Scrum Team. Two specific attributes of the Scrum Team are that they are self-organizing and cross-functional. The Scrum Guide explains that "Self-organizing teams choose how best to accomplish their work, rather than being directed by others outside the team. Cross-functional teams have all competencies needed to accomplish the work without depending on others not part of the team."[37] In addition, Scrum Teams are expected to "deliver products iteratively and incrementally maximizing opportunities for feedback."[38] These are major responsibilities of the Scrum Team. Not only are they expected to deliver products, but they are expected to operate in a self-organizing and cross-functional manner. These are challenging things to do. And that's why I concur with the creators of Scrum when they say that Scrum is "lightweight, simple to understand, and difficult to master."[39] As an Agilist, my responsibilities include coaching the Development Team in self-organization and cross-functionality. My ability to effectively do this requires that I understand and apply strategic practices that will subtly and organically push the team in this direction. No pressure. Instead of looking at my responsibilities as pressure, I'm now starting to look at them as opportunities. I can now explore, identify, and implement practical suggestions to help me and other Agilists in the arduous task of coaching Scrum Team members to be self-organizing and cross-functional.

The terms *Self-Organizing* and *Cross-Functional* can be defined respectively as:

- Self-Organizing: Reflects the management philosophy whereby operational decisions are delegated as much as possible to those who have the most detailed knowledge of the consequences and practicalities associated with those decisions.[40]
- Cross-Functional: A team composed of members with all the functional skills (such as UI designers, developers, testers) and specialties necessary to complete work that requires more than a single discipline.[41]

One of the authors that has helped me learn how to lead teams is John Maxwell. Maxwell wrote a book titled *The 17 Essential Qualities of a Team Player.* In the introduction of the book, Maxwell says "When it comes to having good people on a team, you really have only two choices: train them or trade for them. You grow the players you already have into champions, or you go out and recruit championship-caliber people and bring them onto the team."[42] My goal as an Agilist was to read and understand the qualities described in this book, and then identify some practical ways for how Agilists can apply these principles within their Scrum team. Following are the seventeen qualities that were outlined in Maxwell's book and a separate column with some practices I've identified for how these principles can be carried out by an Agilist.

"The 17 Qualities and Practices"

No.	Qualities	Practices
1.	**Adaptable** "If you won't change for the team, the team may change you."[43] Defined: Able to adjust to new conditions; specifically adapting yourself to the team.[44] Why should team members be adaptable? In a software project, priorities can change at any time and sometimes requiring that team member step out of their specialized roles to help the team meet their objectives. The team needs to be adaptable and operate under these changed conditions.	a. To become more adaptable, team members should always re-evaluate their roles: Ask developers/BAs/testers to re-evaluate their roles to get involved in other areas that's outside of their specialized roles. Explain to them that to become a self-organized team, team members need to be willing to adapt themselves to the team, not for the team to adapt to them. b. Encourage team members to be more service-minded. We're encouraging them to get to a place of sacrificing their own comfort for the sake of the team. See examples of athletes that have done that. Maybe pick an example from these selfless stories and speak about it at the next retrospective: - "Kirk Gibson Hobbles His Way to a Home Run" - Willis Reed Inspires the Knicks All the Way to an NBA Championship - Jack Youngblood Plays with a Fractured Fibula - Kerri Strug Sticks an Unexpected Landing"[45] c. Encourage your organizations to hire professionals (specifically the development team) that are willing to step out of their specialized roles. This should be discussed in interviews and specified in job descriptions.

2.	**Collaborative**
	
	"Working together precedes winning together."[46]
	
	Defined: Cooperation is working together agreeably; while collaboration is working together aggressively.[47]
	
	Why should team members be collaborative?
	
	Agile teams are expected to self-organize and create the architecture and design for solutions.
		a. Meet with the key influencers on the team and encourage them to take themselves out of the picture; specifically encourage them to propose ideas that promote and involve people other than themselves.
		b. Encourage team members to compliment and complement each other.
		  i. Try an exercise for complimenting each other: i.e. an activity in which team members appreciate each other's contributions by offering intangible thank you.
		  ii. Try an Exercise for how to complement each other: Conduct one on one with team members and ask what areas they would like to improve in. Once you've that information, confirm if there's anyone on the team that can help the team member in that area. This allows people with complementary gifts to work together.

3.	**Committed** "There are no half-hearted champions."[48] Defined: Pledged or bound to a certain course or policy; dedicated[49] Why should team members be committed?	a. Create working agreement: Teams can sustain commitments when they're based on solid values. These values are like (1) glue (2) a foundation (3) a ruler (4) a compass (5) a magnet and (6) an identity. There are many exercises to use to help teams discuss and establish shared values.[50]

	Agile teams are expected to be self-organized and self-directing. They're committed to meeting specific goals in each sprint.	
4.	**Communicative** "A team is many voices with a single heart."[51] Defined: Willing, eager, or able to talk or impart information[52] Why should team members be communicative? In Agile, the business personnel and development team work closely together. It's imperative for the development team to be able to communicate the technical implications of a business decision; it's just as important for the business to be able to communicate the business implications of a technical decision.	a. Secure a commitment from leaders to be authentic and transparent. This breaks down the intimidation factor between leaders and the rest of the team. b. Help leaders and team members talk to and listen to each other. i. Create shared values or team agreements: By understanding each other's values, you'll gain insight of what you can do to build trust, respect and communication with that person. c. Equip team members to know about each other, and about the team's goals and methods. The more they know, the more they'll understand. The more they understand, the more they'll care. d. Understand goals: Have someone (with clout in the organization) other than the product owner periodically share the importance and value of the work the team is doing. This can be done during the parking lot of a daily standup, at a planning session, or whatever time that works for the team. e. Interact with each other: Use the M.Y. N.A.M.E exercise in *Quick Team-Building Activities for Busy Managers.*[53]

5.	**Competent** "If you can't, your team won't."[54] Defined: Having the necessary ability, knowledge, or skill to do something successfully.[55] Why should team members be competent? One of the principles of Agile is to build projects around motivated individuals. Give them the environment and support that they need and trust them to get the job done. The key part in the principle is for the team to "...get the job done." If you do not possess the necessary skill set then you cannot get the job done.	a. Highly competent people are (1) committed to excellence (2) never settle for average (3) pay attention to detail and (4) perform with consistency. To help someone to become more competent, you need to help them to focus professionally. i. Evaluate their experience, skills, temperament, attitude, passion, people skills, discipline, emotional strength, and potential. ii. Meet with the person's supervisor/manager to confirm how they're assessing the person's performance. If they have something in place, coordinate with them. iii. If there's no assessment in place, express the concerns you're having to them and to their manager and work on an improvement plan (PIP). Periodically assess that plan to see how the team member is improving. iv. Ask the tech-lead (who is doing the code review of the developer) to give an assessment of the individual's performance.
6.	**Dependable** "Teams go to Go-To players."[56] Defined: Trustworthy and reliable.[57]	a. Character + Competence + Commitment + Consistency + Cohesion = Dependability b. As the leader, you can engage undependable team members with the following questions. These questions can generate insight, which can then become the launching pad to offer suggestions to help the person improve in these areas.

	Why should team members be dependable? Agile team members must be dependable. Since there's less command-control on Agile teams, team members are self-organized and are expected to take more ownership of their work. An undependable team member can put the sprint and release goals at risk.	i. Is your integrity questioned? (character) ii. Do you perform your work with excellence? How can the team tell? (competence) iii. Are you dedicated to the team's success? How can the team tell? (commitment) iv. Can you be depended on every time? Are there areas where you're not consistent? (consistency)? v. Do your actions bring the team together (cohesion)?
7.	**Disciplined** "What we do on some great occasion will probably depend on what we already are; and what we are will be the result of previous years of self-discipline."[58] Defined: Showing a controlled form of behavior or way of working.[59] Why should Agile teams be disciplined? Agile teams are expected to deliver valuable software every 2-4 weeks in a time-boxed period called a sprint. In that time-boxed period, Agile teams	a. Take on challenges: Encourage team members to pick a task or project that will put them in over their head. Doing this will require them to think sharply and act with discipline. To encourage employees to do the following: i. Ask the employee this question: "In what other ways do you feel you can contribute to this team? Is there anything you would like to learn that you're not learning?" b. Before meeting with a developer/tester, meet with their supervisor/manager to find out if there's anything they feel the individual can improve upon. Having this insight gives you an idea of some challenges you can suggest that would be outside of their comfort zone.

	are working towards a sprint goal while effectively managing distractions. To consistently meet the sprint goals, the team must be disciplined (i.e. controlled) in how they manage sprint goals and distractions.	
8.	**Enlarging** "Adding value to teammates is invaluable"[60] Defined: Enlarging is when individuals are intentional about helping team members go to another level; intentional about adding value to their team members and valuing what their team members value. Why should Agile teams be enlarging? Agile Principle #11 notes that the best requirements and architecture emerge from self-organizing teams. The act of enlarging is a behavior that will help to sustain the autonomy of the team.	a. Enlargers value their teammates. Sharing positive observations of teammates can show that you believe in them, and "if you believe in others and give them a positive reputation to uphold, you can help them to become better than they think they are."[61] i. For each retrospective, set apart time to do "Kudos" - this is a recognition activity in which peers and not their boss, appreciate the participants. If you're using an interactive tool (i.e. noteapp), you can just create a section titled "Kudos." Using this game is a subtle way of encouraging team members to begin enlarging each other.

9.	**Enthusiastic**	a. If you're dealing with a team member that is unenthusiastic, encourage them to be willing to do more.
	"Your heart is the source of energy for the team. There is no substitute for enthusiasm. When members of a team are enthusiastic, the whole team becomes highly energized"[62]	b. In your one on one with them, instruct that team member: "This week (or sprint), when someone asks you to do something, do what's required and then some. Then quietly observe its impact on the team's atmosphere."
	Defined: Having or showing intense and eager enjoyment, interest or approval.[63]	
	Why should Agile teams be enthusiastic?	
	Agile teams are built around trusted and motivated individuals. Helping individuals to become more enthusiastic will energize the whole team, thereby creating an atmosphere that fuels motivation.	
10.	**Intentional**	a. Plan your calendar with purpose: We want to encourage team members to plan long term periods with intentionality. We want to help our team members to plan our activities in a longer block. Planning in longer blocks helps us to be more intentional throughout our days.
	"You've got to think about the 'big things' while you're doing small things, so that all the small things go in the right direction"[64]	

	Defined: It's about focusing on doing the right things, moment to moment, day to day, and then following through with them in a consistent way.[65] Why should Agile teams be intentional? Agile teams are generally focused on meeting the specific goals of a sprint. To effectively do this, team members must be intentional, intensely focusing on the planning and the execution of the right things.	i. To practically help your team member do this, engage them in a one on one. In your one on one, ask them the following: 1. "What are your top priorities?" You should expect them to say something that's consistent with the sprint goals. 2. "What are some of the things that are breaking your flow of work (i.e. scatters)?" Once they identify them, work with the team member to help resolve these scatters. ii. To help at the team level, ask team members at the next retrospective to list a dozen scatters affecting the team.
11.	**Mission-Conscious** "He who has a 'why' to live for can bear almost any 'how.'"[66] Defined: Full awareness of how your efforts are contributing to the completion of a bigger effort. Why should Agile teams be mission-conscious?	a. As the team leader, ensure that you're constantly mentioning the purpose of the release. Mention it at least twice a week during the daily standups. b. Have someone with clout in the organization (other than the PO) periodically share the purpose of the release. This can be done during the parking lot of a daily standup or at a planning session, or whatever time that works for the team.

	Continuous delivery of valuable software is the expectation for an Agile team. The product or services being delivered is typically the component of an overall mission. It's important they understand this mission they're helping to achieve. The understanding of this mission can help team members develop a sense of purpose prompting them to always do what's best for the cause.	
12.	**Prepared** "Preparation can make the difference between winning and losing."[67] Defined: properly expectant, organized, or equipped; ready[68] Why should Agile teams be prepared? For Agile teams to be successful, team members must trust each other to get the job done. Part of that job is coming to Scrum ceremonies prepared. For example, team members	a. If you notice that a team member is consistently unprepared, use your one-on-one time with him/her to discuss this concern. One way to help the person is to encourage them to create some type of a system (i.e. check-list) that will help them to stay focused and less distracted.

	must come to the daily meetings prepared to answer the three questions. A lack of preparation can lead to unproductive discussions and inefficient collaborations, consequently reducing the likelihood for the team to meet their sprint goals.	
13.	**Relational** "If you get along, others will go along."[69] Defined: concerning the way in which two or more people or things are connected.[70] Why should Agile teams be relational? One of the values of Agile is: Interaction and individuals over process and tools. We clearly see that projects are facilitated by people, not tools; and problems get resolved by people. Clearly, there's a people aspect to Agile we cannot ignore.	a. Ask the right questions: encourage team members to learn about each other's hopes, desires and goals. For example, if you have 10 members on a team, task five of the team members to reach out to the assigned team members to ask them the following: i. What is one thing that many people don't know about you?" ii. Use the retrospective to get feedback from the team members. iii. As team member A shares information about team member B, ask team member B how they got into that specific thing.

	Consequently, the success of an Agile team is based on the quality of the relationships amongst the team.	
14.	**Self-Improving** "To improve the team improve yourself."[71] Defined: The practice of improving one's knowledge, status, or character by one's own efforts.[72] Why should Agile teams be self-improving? Agile Principle #12 states: At regular intervals, the team reflects on how to become more effective, then tunes and adjusts its behavior accordingly. When individuals on the team improve themselves, they are automatically improving the overall team and its likelihood for success.	a. Encourage team members to be highly teachable - you can do this by encouraging them to take on new disciplines and new tasks during the sprint. b. Meet with the person's supervisor/manager to confirm how they're assessing the person's annual performance. If they have something in place, coordinate with them.

15.	**Selfless**	a. Promote someone other than yourself – "if you are in the habit of talking up your achievement and promoting yourself to others, determine to keep silent about yourself and praise others for 2 weeks."[75]
	"There is no 'I' in team"[73]	
	Defined: Concerned more with the needs and wishes of others than with one's own; unselfish.[74]	i. For each retrospective, set apart time to do "Kudos" - this is a recognition activity in which peers and not their boss, appreciate the participants. If you are using an interactive tool (i.e. noteapp), you can just create a section titled "Kudos." You can use this time to say positive things about people's actions and qualities.
	Why should Agile teams be self-less?	
	To ensure success in an Agile team, team members will sometimes have to put others on the team ahead of themselves. There are times when team members are going to have to promote someone other than themselves. This selfless behavior can help improve/motivate others, thereby improving the overall team.	
16.	**Solution-Oriented**	a. If you notice a team member that struggles in this area, help them to either refocus their thinking or rethink their strategy. A good way to address this issue is via one on one. In your one on one with the individual, ask them to walk through their approach in solving the problem. Coach them to use the following questions when trying to (1) Understand the problem (2) solve the problem and (3) evaluate the decision.
	"Make a resolution to find the solution"[76]	
	Defined: These individuals recognize that problems are a matter of perspective; and sense that all problems or challenges are solvable.	
	Why should Agile teams be solution-oriented?	

	Agile teams must be solution oriented. The basis for their work is oftentimes finding a "solution" for a business problem. In some organizations, priorities are always shifting (and new business problems are always emerging), Agile teams should operate with the approach that: (1) problems are a matter of perspective and (2) all problems are solvable.	i. Understand the problem
		  1. Have you defined the problem in your own words?
		  2. Are you clear about what you are trying to do? Where are you now and where do you want to get to?
		ii. Solve the problem
		  1. Have you checked your assumptions?
		  2. Out of all the possible solutions, have you identified a list of the feasible ones?
		  3. Has anyone else faced this problem? How did they solve it?
		iii. Evaluate the decision
		  1. Have you checked your solution from all angles?
		  2. Is the plan realistic?
		  3. Do you have a plan with dates or times for completion?

17.	**Tenacious** "Never, never, never quit."[77] Defined: persistent in maintaining, adhering to, or seeking something valued or desired.[78] Why should Agile teams be tenacious? Agile teams like any other teams must be tenacious if they desire to consistently see success. Making success a common achievement	a. People tend to be tenacious when they stand for something. Helping team-members to be more mission-conscious, can prompt them to give all that they have and to work with determination. Consider the following suggestions: i. As the team leader, ensure that you're constantly mentioning the purpose of the release...i.e. mention it at least twice a week during the daily standups. b. Have someone with clout in the organization (other than the PO) periodically share the purpose of the release. This can be done during the parking lot of a daily standup or at a

and striving for technical excellence will emerge from teams that work with determination and are intentional about giving all that they have.	planning session, or whatever time that works for the team.

Endnotes

Introduction

[1]   Gaiyasudeen Syed, *Who is an Agilist?*, accessed July, 2017, https://www. linkedin.com/pulse/who-agilist-dr-gaiyasudeen-syed.

[2]   Gallup, *State of the American Workplace*, accessed July 2017, https:// www.gallup.com/workplace/238085/state-american-workplace-report-2017.aspx.

Chapter 1: Purpose of an Agilist

[3]   Myles Munroe, *Spirit of Leadership* (New Kensington, PA: Whitaker House, 2005), 52.

[4]   Munroe, *Spirit of Leadership*, 56.

[5]   Munroe, *Spirit of Leadership*, 57.

[6]   Munroe, *Spirit of Leadership*, 62.

[7]   Munroe, *Spirit of Leadership*, 229.

[8]   Myles Munroe, *In Pursuit of Purpose* (Shippensburg, PA: Destiny Image, 1992), 103.

Chapter 2: Conviction of an Agilist

[9]   Myles Munroe, *Spirit of Leadership*, 55.

[10]   2 Cor. 11:23-27, NIV.

[11]   Robert Herbold, *What's Holding You Back: 10 Bold Steps that Define Gutsy Leaders* (San Francisco: Jossey-Bass, 2011), 6.

[12]   Herbold, *What's Holding You Back: 10 Bold Steps that Define Gutsy Leaders*,14.

[13]   Brad Lomenick, *H3 Leadership* (Nashville: Nelson Books, 2015), 34.

Chapter 3: Vision of an Agilist

[14] Prov. 29:18, NIV.

[15] Stephen Covey, *The 7 Habits of Highly Effective People* (New York: Simon and Schuster, 2013), 105.

[16] John Maxwell, *Developing the Leader Within You Workbook* (Nashville: Thomas Nelson, 2001), 171.

Chapter 4: Passion of an Agilist

[17] Myles Munroe, *Spirit of Leadership*, 228.

[18] Brad Lomenick, *H3 Leadership*, 83.

[19] National Institute of Mental Health, *Social Anxiety Disorder: More Than Just Shyness* (Bethesda, MD: 2016), 3-4.

[20] Ian Tuhovsky, *The Science of Effective Communication: Improve Your Social Skills and Small Talk, Develop Charisma and Learn How to Talk to Anyone* (Scotts Valley, CA: CreateSpace Independent Publishing Platform, 2017), 1.

[21] Edward Welch, *What Do You Think of Me? Why Do I Care?* (Greensboro, NC: New Growth Press, 2011), 129-130.

[22] Welch, *What Do You Think of Me? Why Do I Care?*, 131.

[23] Tuhovsky, *The Science of Effective Communication: Improve Your Social Skills and Small Talk, Develop Charisma and Learn How to Talk to Anyone*, 7-8.

Chapter 5: The Inspiring Agilist

[24] *Oxford Living Dictionary*, s.v. "Inspire," accessed July, 2018, https://en.oxforddictionaries.com/definition/inspire.

[25] Rosabeth Kanter, *"Ten Reasons People Resist Change,"* accessed July, 2018, https://hbr.org/2012/09/ten-reasons-people-resist-change.

[26] Myles Munroe, *Spirit of Leadership*, 53.

[27] Munroe, *Spirit of Leadership*, 54.

[28] Robert Kellemen, *Soul Physicians* (Winona Lake, IN: BMH Books, 2007) 201.

[29] Munroe, *Spirit of Leadership*, 53.

[30] Agility in Mind. (n.d.). Case Study: Route-to-Market Efficiencies for RSA Global Digital Teams, accessed July 2018, https://www.agilityinmind.com/case-studies/rsa/.

[31] Agility in Mind. (n.d.). Case Study: Route-to-Market Efficiencies for RSA Global Digital Teams, accessed July, 2018, https://www.agilityinmind.com/case-studies/rsa/.

[32] Mann, C. and F. Maurer. *A Case Study on the Impact of Scrum on Overtime and Customer Satisfaction.*, accessed July, 2018, ResearchGate, 10.

[33] Mann, C. and F. Maurer. *A Case Study on the Impact of Scrum on Overtime and Customer Satisfaction.*, accessed July, 2018, ResearchGate, 10.

[34] Mann, C. and F. Maurer. *A Case Study on the Impact of Scrum on Overtime and Customer Satisfaction.*, accessed July, 2018, ResearchGate, 9.

[35] Mann, C. and F. Maurer. *A Case Study on the Impact of Scrum on Overtime and Customer Satisfaction.*, accessed July, 2018, ResearchGate, 9.

Appendix A: In Pursuit of Self-Organization via Scrum

[36] Schwaber, Ken and Jeff Sutherland. *The Scrum Guide. The Definitive Guide to Scrum: The Rules of the Game,* accessed August 2107, Scrum.org, 3.

[37] Schwaber, Ken and Jeff Sutherland. *The Scrum Guide. The Definitive Guide to Scrum: The Rules of the Game,* accessed August 2107, Scrum.org, 6.

[38] Schwaber, Ken and Jeff Sutherland. *The Scrum Guide. The Definitive Guide to Scrum: The Rules of the Game,* accessed August 2107, Scrum.org, 6.

[39] Schwaber, Ken and Jeff Sutherland. *The Scrum Guide. The Definitive Guide to Scrum: The Rules of the Game,* accessed August 2107, Scrum.org, 3.

[40] Kenneth Rubin, *Essential Scrum. A Practical Guide to the Most Popular Agile Process* (Upper Saddle River, NJ: Pearson Education Inc., 2013), 416.

[41] Rubin, *Essential Scrum. A Practical Guide to the Most Popular Agile Process,* 405.

[42] John Maxwell, *The Essential Qualities of a Team Player* (Nashville: Thomas Nelson, Inc., 2002), xi.

[43] Maxwell, *The Essential Qualities of a Team Player,* 1.

[44] *Oxford Living Dictionary*, s.v. "Adaptable," accessed June, 2019, https://en.oxforddictionaries.com/definition/adaptable.

[45] Tony Markovich. *Athletes Who Sacrificed Their Own Game for the Good of the Team*, accessed June 2017, https://www.complex.com/sports/2016/01/10-athletes-who-sacrificed-their-own-game-for-the-good-of-the-team/.

[46] Maxwell, *The Essential Qualities of a Team Player*, 10.

[47] Maxwell, *The Essential Qualities of a Team Player*, 13.

[48] Maxwell, *The Essential Qualities of a Team Player*, 19.

[49] *Oxford Living Dictionary*, s.v. "Committed," accessed June 2, 2019, https://en.oxforddictionaries.com/definition/committed.

[50] Dhaval Panchal. *Sharing Values, an Agile Team-Building Exercise*, accessed June 2017, https://www.solutionsiq.com/resource/blog-post/sharing-values-an-agile-team-building-exercise/.

[51] Maxwell, *The Essential Qualities of a Team Player*, 28.

[52] *Oxford Living Dictionary*, s.v. "Communicative," accessed June 2019, https://en.oxforddictionaries.com/definition/communicative.

[53] Brian Miller, *Quick Team Building Activities for Busy Managers* (Broadway, NY: American Management Association, 1956), 62.

[54] Maxwell, *The Essential Qualities of a Team Player*, 37.

[55] *Oxford Living Dictionary*, s.v. "Competent," accessed June 2019, https://en.oxforddictionaries.com/definition/competent.

[56] Maxwell, *The Essential Qualities of a Team Player*, 46.

[57] *Oxford Living Dictionary*, s.v. "Dependable," accessed June 2019, https://en.oxforddictionaries.com/definition/dependable.

[58] Maxwell, *The Essential Qualities of a Team Player*, 55.

[59] *Oxford Living Dictionary*, s.v. "Disciplined," accessed June 2019, https://en.oxforddictionaries.com/definition/disciplined.

[60] Maxwell, *The Essential Qualities of a Team Player*, 63.

[61] Maxwell, *The Essential Qualities of a Team Player*, 78.

[62] Maxwell, *The Essential Qualities of a Team Player*, 71.

[63] *Oxford Living Dictionary*, s.v. "Enthusiastic," accessed June 2019, https://en.oxforddictionaries.com/definition/enthusiastic.

[64] Maxwell, *The Essential Qualities of a Team Player*, 80.

[65] Maxwell, *The Essential Qualities of a Team Player*, 83.

[66] Maxwell, *The Essential Qualities of a Team Player*, 89.

[67] Maxwell, *The Essential Qualities of a Team Player*, 98.

[68] Dictionary.com, s.v. "Prepared," accessed on June 2019, https://www.dictionary.com/browse/prepared.

[69] Maxwell, *The Essential Qualities of a Team Player*, 107.

[70] Oxford Living Dictionary, s.v. "Relational," accessed June 2019, https://en.oxforddictionaries.com/definition/relational.

[71] Maxwell, *The Essential Qualities of a Team Player*, 116.

[72] Oxford Living Dictionary, s.v. "Self-improvement," accessed June 2019, https://en.oxforddictionaries.com/definition/self-improvement.

[73] Maxwell, *The Essential Qualities of a Team Player*, 125.

[74] Oxford Living Dictionary, s.v. "Selfless," accessed June 2, 2019, https://en.oxforddictionaries.com/definition/selfless.

[75] Maxwell, *The Essential Qualities of a Team Player*, 131-32.

[76] Maxwell, *The Essential Qualities of a Team Player*, 134.

[77] Maxwell, *The Essential Qualities of a Team Player*, 141.

[78] Merriam Webster, s.v. "Tenacious," accessed June 2019, https://www.merriam-webster.com/dictionary/tenacious .